WEATHER MAKES THEM MOVE

ELEPHANT MIGRATION

by Rachel Rose

Consultant: Beth Gambro
Reading Specialist, Yorkville, Illinois

Minneapolis, Minnesota

Teaching Tips

Before Reading
- Look at the cover of the book. Discuss the picture and the title.
- Ask readers to brainstorm a list of what they already know about elephants. What can they expect to see in this book?
- Go on a picture walk, looking through the pictures to discuss vocabulary and make predictions about the text.

During Reading
- Read for purpose. Encourage readers to think about elephant movement as they are reading.
- Ask readers to look for the details of the book. Why do elephants migrate?
- If readers encounter an unknown word, ask them to look at the sounds in the word. Then, ask them to look at the rest of the page. Are there any clues to help them understand?

After Reading
- Encourage readers to pick a buddy and reread the book together.
- Ask readers to name a reason elephants move. Find a page that tells about this thing.
- Ask readers to write or draw something they learned about elephant migration.

Copyright © 2024 Bearport Publishing Company. All rights reserved. No part of this publication may be reproduced in whole or in part, stored in any retrieval system, or transmitted in any form or by any means, electronic, mechanical, photocopying, recording, or otherwise, without written permission from the publisher.

For more information, write to Bearport Publishing, 5357 Penn Avenue South, Minneapolis, MN 55419.

Library of Congress Cataloging-in-Publication Data

Names: Rose, Rachel, 1968- author.
Title: Elephant migration / by Rachel Rose.
Description: Minneapolis, Minnesota : Bearport Publishing, [2024] | Series: Weather makes them move | Includes bibliographical references and index.
Identifiers: LCCN 2022059173 (print) | LCCN 2022059174 (ebook) | ISBN 9798888220665 (hardcover) | ISBN 9798888223819 (ebook)
Subjects: LCSH: Elephants--Migration--Juvenile literature. | Elephants--Seasonal distribution--Juvenile literature.
Classification: LCC QL737.P98 R67 2024 (print) | LCC QL737.P98 (ebook) | DDC 599/.6713--dc23/eng/20221215
LC record available at https://lccn.loc.gov/2022059173
LC ebook record available at https://lccn.loc.gov/2022059174

Credits:
Cover and title page, © Rixipix/iStock; 3, © gualtiero boffi/Shutterstock; 5, © JeffGrabert/iStock; 7, © AndreAnita/Shutterstock; 8–9, © David Steele/Shutterstock; 11, © Kathryn Shutterstock; 12–13, © KenCanning/iStock; 15, © Benny Marty/Shutterstock; 16–17, © Villiers Steyn/Shutterstock; 18–19, © GomezDavid/iStock; 20–21, © johan63/iStock; 22T, © stuporter/Adobe Stock; 22M, © Ondrej Prosicky/Shutterstock; 22B, © Jonathan Pledger/Shutterstock; 23TL, © Henk Bogaard/Shutterstock; 23TR, © Title Image Production/Shutterstock; 23BL, © dvrcan/Adobe Stock; 23BR, © Volodymyr Burdiak/Shutterstock.

Contents

Follow the Leader 4

On the Move! 22

Glossary 23

Index 24

Read More 24

Learn More Online...................... 24

About the Author 24

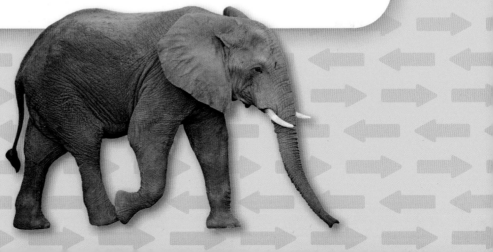

Follow the Leader

A group of elephants is on the move!

The oldest one leads the way.

The rest follow.

Where are they going?

Say elephants like EL-uh-fuhnts

There are a few kinds of elephants.

Some live in the dry **savannas** of Africa.

These are the biggest elephants.

Savanna elephants live in family groups.

Often, the oldest mother leads the **herd**.

Herds spend most of their time eating.

Elephants eat grasses and leaves.

Sometimes, they munch on branches.

They need a lot of food.

11

The savannas have two **seasons**.

One is rainy.

It is called the wet season.

Plenty of food grows for hungry elephants.

13

Then, the rain stops.

Food runs out without the water.

This is the dry season.

Elephants must leave to find more food and water.

Luckily, they have good **memories**.

Elephants know where they can find water.

They can go there for food, too.

After a while, the seasons change again.

The wet season starts.

This means the elephants can go home.

Every year, elephants make this trip.

And it is all because the weather makes them move!

On the Move!

Migration (mye-GRAY-shuhn) is when animals move from one place to another. Often, they travel far. Let's learn more about savanna elephant migration!

Savanna elephants usually leave their homes sometime between June and November.

They usually return anytime from October to June.

Elephants can remember places to find water for more than 10 years.

Glossary

herd a large group of elephants

memories abilities to keep thoughts about things from the past

savannas large, open areas of land where grasses and bushes grow

seasons different times during the year with different weather

Index

dry 6, 14
eating 10
food 10, 12, 14, 16
herd 8, 10

rain 12, 14
seasons 12, 14, 18
water 14, 16, 22
wet 12, 18

Read More

Duling, Kaitlyn. *African Elephants (Animals of the Grasslands).* Minneapolis: Bellwether Media, 2020.

Huddleston, Emma. *Asian Elephants (Save the Animals!).* Minneapolis: Bearport Publishing Company, 2023.

Learn More Online

1. Go to **www.factsurfer.com** or scan the QR code below.
2. Enter **"Elephant Migration"** into the search box.
3. Click on the cover of this book to see a list of websites.

About the Author

Rachel Rose is a writer who lives in California. One day, she hopes to visit the African savannas and see the elephants there.